LOOK-ALIKE
BIRDS

LOOK-ALIKE BIRDS

How to tell them apart

Kenneth Newman
Derek Solomon

Illustrations by Jenny Preston

SOUTHERN
BOOK PUBLISHERS

ISBN 1 86812 519 X

First edition, first impression 1994

Published by
Southern Book Publishers (Pty) Ltd
PO Box 3103, Halfway House, 1685

Cover illustration and cartoon on p. 2 by Dr Jack
Illustrations by Jenny Preston
Set in 10 on 12 pt Palatino
Typesetting and reproduction by PG&A, Wetton, Cape
Printed and bound by National Book Printers, Goodwood, Cape

CONTENTS

INTRODUCTION

This book has been designed as one of several supplements to *Newman's Birds of Southern Africa*. In 1992 Ken Newman published *Beating About the Bush*, a book designed to help novice birdwatchers set about birding in the right way – it gives advice on choosing binoculars, on deciding where to go birding and on what you need to look at when you see a bird in order to identify it. It also has helpful notes on some identification problems. *Look-Alike Birds* follows on where *Beating About the Bush* left off.

In 1991 Derek Solomon first published *Bundukit*, a book aimed at helping Zimbabwean birders distinguish between local birds of similar appearance. Together Ken Newman and Derek Solomon have expanded on the original idea to create *Look-Alike Birds* which details 99 look-alike groups of birds from all over southern Africa.

The correct identification of birds, often in far from ideal circumstances, is a problem that is common to all birdwatchers. *Look-Alike Birds* illustrates a series of common problem species-pairs or groups that cause confusion throughout the southern African subregion. The object is to provide a few critical keys for each species, ignoring all features that are shared with its look-alike. To this end the illustrations have been deliberately simplified. Pointers and comparisons between species are the core of the system. In certain cases the restricted locality of a species form an important part of its identification, and maps highlighting these restricted distributions help to solve the problems.

Terms and abbreviations used in this guide

BAND	A horizontal stripe, often black; e.g. breast-band, tailband.
BR.	Breeding.
CAP	Top of the head from the eye upwards.
CASQUE	A horny extension on top of the bill as seen in some hornbills.
CERE	Fleshy section between beak and face; seen in raptors, pigeons and parrots.
CHEEK	The face below the eye.
COVERTS	Feathers that serve as covers; e.g. ear coverts.
CREST	Elongated head feathers.
CROWN	Top of the head.
CULMEN	The top ridge of the beak.
DECURVED	Bent downwards (as in decurved beak).
EYEBROW	Horizontal line of colour above the eye.
EYE-STRIPE	A line, often black, running through the eye from lores to ear coverts.
FLANKS	Sides of the body below the folded wing.
FRONTAL SHIELD	A fleshy plate on the forehead of some waterbirds.
GAPE	The corner of the mouth forming the hinge of the upper and lower mandibles.
HOOD	A head cap, often black, that extends to below the eyes.
LORES	The point between eye and beak.
MANTLE	The upper back.
NAPE	The upper hind neck.
N-BR.	Non-breeding.
PRIMARIES	The major wing feathers on the outer part of a bird's wing; primary feathers.
RUFOUS	Reddish-brown.
RUMP	The lower back above the tail base.
SECONDARIES	Secondary wing feathers; those between the primaries and the bird's body.
SIDEBURNS	A term used to describe the dark patch on the side of a falcon's head.
STREAMERS	Slender tail extensions as seen in swallows and bee-eaters.
TARSUS	The lower leg.
TARSAL JOINT	The leg joint between upper and lower leg (often erroneously called the knee).
UNDERPARTS	The under body of a bird.
VENT	The undertail coverts.
WATTLES	Bare fleshy structure around the eye or near the base of the bill in some birds.
WINDOWS	Describes the transparent patches in the white wings of some birds when seen in flight.
WING-BAR	A horizontal bar of colour on a bird's wing.

HOW TO USE THIS BOOK

The 99 look-alike groups in this guide are all keyed to the pages where the species is described in *Newman's Birds of Southern Africa*. This book should therefore be used in conjunction with the fieldguide so that reference can be made to the colour illustrations and the full written descriptions of each species.

Look-Alike Birds is designed to be used as follows: once you have narrowed down the identification of a species to two or three of the species using *Newman's Birds*, turn to the relevant page in *Look-Alike Birds* (birds are listed in the same order as they occur in *Newman's Birds* in the Contents and in alphabetical order in the Index). Here you will find much simplified drawings of the birds in question, highlighting only the points where the birds differ. Pointers on the illustrations and a few succinct lines of text make the distinguishing features easy to isolate. Distribution maps have been included with a few species where the location of a bird is particularly useful in identification, but always remember to check the distribution maps in *Newman's Birds*. If you have looked carefully enough at the bird you will be able to reach an accurate conclusion about its identity.

Using *Look-Alike Birds* will train you to focus on the most important identifying points when you see a bird that could be confused with another similar species.

"IT HELPS WITH VERY CLOSE INSPECTIONS!"

ARCTIC TERN (N-BR)
(Newman's Birds p. 58)

IN FLIGHT LOOK FOR:
1. Mostly white underwing primaries
2. White rump and tail
3. Shorter bill than Common

COMMON TERN (N-BR)
(Newman's Birds p. 58)

IN FLIGHT LOOK FOR:
1. Pearl-grey underwing primaries with dark edges
2. Grey rump and tail
3. Longer bill than Arctic

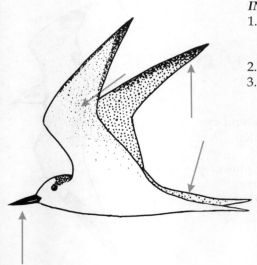

WHISKERED TERN (N-BR)

(*Newman's Birds* p. 60)

LOOK FOR:
1. Broad dark line from eye to nape and speckled rear crown
2. Bill about length of head
3. In flight uniform grey upperwing, tail and rump

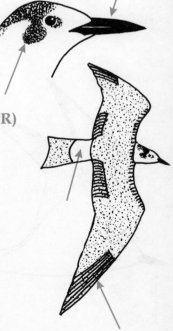

WHITEWINGED TERN (N-BR)

(*Newman's Birds* p. 60)

LOOK FOR:
1. Dark patch below/behind eye extending to rear crown
2. Bill shorter than head
3. In flight white rump plus grey upperwings with darker primaries and secondaries

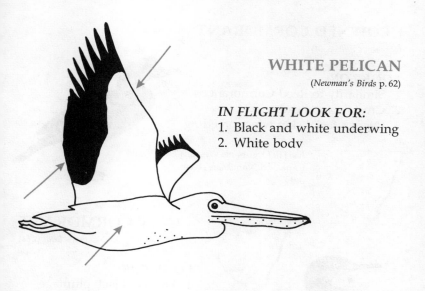

WHITE PELICAN
(Newman's Birds p. 62)

IN FLIGHT LOOK FOR:
1. Black and white underwing
2. White body

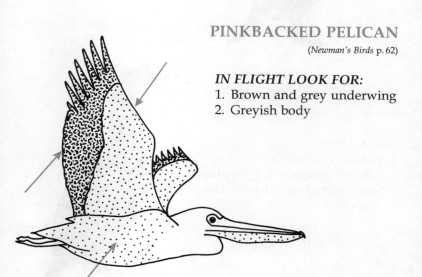

PINKBACKED PELICAN
(Newman's Birds p. 62)

IN FLIGHT LOOK FOR:
1. Brown and grey underwing
2. Greyish body

CROWNED CORMORANT

(Newman's Birds p. 64)

LOOK FOR:
1. Similarity to Reed Cormorant
2. Crest on forehead
3. Orange facial skin when breeding

NOTE: Occurs on Western Cape and Namibian coasts only

CAPE CORMORANT

(Newman's Birds p. 64)

LOOK FOR:
1. Entirely black plumage
2. Orange/yellow skin at base of bill
3. Groups flying in long lines over sea

NOTE: Cape and Bank Cormorants occur only on the Cape and West coasts

BANK CORMORANT

(Newman's Birds p. 64)

LOOK FOR:
1. Robust appearance
2. Black plumage and white rump
3. Small groups on offshore islets and rocks

6

WHITEBREASTED CORMORANT
(*Newman's Birds* p. 64)

LOOK FOR:
1. Large size
2. Adult with white breast only
3. Imm. with entirely white underparts

imm.

NOTE: Whitebreasted and Reed Cormorants are most common on inland waters but also frequent the coast in small numbers

REED CORMORANT
(*Newman's Birds* p. 64)

LOOK FOR:
1. Small size
2. Adult entirely blackish
3. Imm. with whitish underparts but more buffy on breast

imm.

GREENBACKED HERON

(Newman's Birds p. 66)

LOOK FOR:
1. Small, grey heron with black hood
2. Dark wing feathers edged white

DWARF BITTERN

(Newman's Birds p. 66)

LOOK FOR:
1. Slate-grey upperparts
2. Buffy, heavily streaked underparts

LITTLE BITTERN (male) ♂

(*Newman's Birds* p. 66)

LOOK FOR:

1. Small buffy heron with black cap, back and tail
2. Whitish wing patches seen at rest and in flight

LITTLE BITTERN (female)

(*Newman's Birds* p. 66)

LOOK FOR:

1. Small, well streaked, buffy heron
2. Cap black, back and tail brown

9

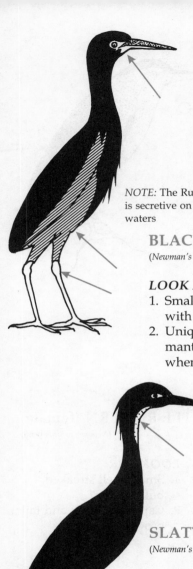

RUFOUSBELLIED HERON
(Newman's Birds p. 66)

LOOK FOR:
1. Small blackish heron with yellow facial skin and legs
2. Dull, red-brown underparts
3. In flight also red-brown tail and inner wing panels

NOTE: The Rufousbellied Heron is secretive on quiet, well-wooded waters

BLACK EGRET
(Newman's Birds p. 68)

LOOK FOR:
1. Small blackish heron with yellow feet
2. Unique habit of mantling its wings when fishing

SLATY EGRET
(Newman's Birds p. 68)

LOOK FOR:
1. Small slate-grey heron with yellow legs and feet
2. Small rufous throat patch

NOTE: These two herons are not secretive

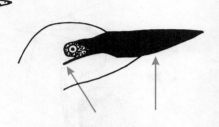

NOTE: The Great White Egret has a black bill for 2–3 weeks when breeding

GREAT WHITE EGRET
(*Newman's Birds* p. 72)

LOOK FOR:
1. Large white heron with long slender neck
2. Long black legs and feet and (normally) yellow bill
3. Gape extending back behind eye

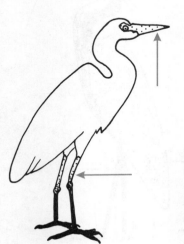

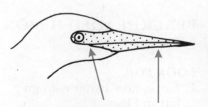

NOTE: The Yellowbilled Egret has an orange-red bill and upper legs for 2–3 weeks when breeding

YELLOWBILLED EGRET
(*Newman's Birds* p. 72)

LOOK FOR:
1. Medium sized white heron with yellow bill
2. Upper legs dull yellow; lower legs and feet black
3. Gape finishing below eye

11

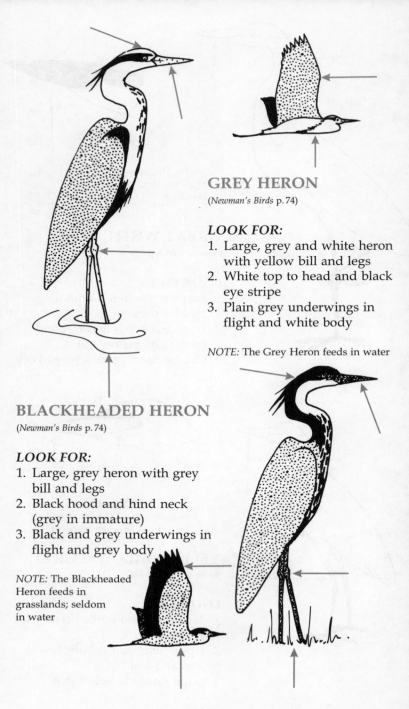

GREY HERON
(*Newman's Birds* p. 74)

LOOK FOR:
1. Large, grey and white heron with yellow bill and legs
2. White top to head and black eye stripe
3. Plain grey underwings in flight and white body

NOTE: The Grey Heron feeds in water

BLACKHEADED HERON
(*Newman's Birds* p. 74)

LOOK FOR:
1. Large, grey heron with grey bill and legs
2. Black hood and hind neck (grey in immature)
3. Black and grey underwings in flight and grey body

NOTE: The Blackheaded Heron feeds in grasslands; seldom in water

BLACK STORK

(Newman's Birds p. 78)

LOOK FOR:
1. Black and white stork with red bill and legs
2. Entirely black upperparts in flight
3. In flight feet protrude beyond tail more than in Abdim's Stork

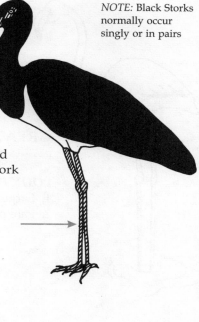

NOTE: Black Storks normally occur singly or in pairs

ABDIM'S STORK

(Newmans Birds p. 78)

LOOK FOR:
1. Black and white stork with tawny bill, blue facial skin
2. Pink legs; red tarsal joints
3. In flight shows white rump and lower back
4. In flight feet protrude less beyond tail than in Black Stork

NOTE: Abdim's Storks normally occur in flocks

13

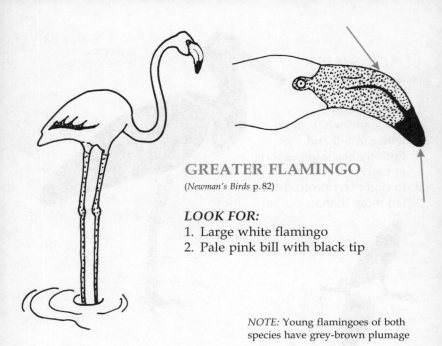

GREATER FLAMINGO

(*Newman's Birds* p. 82)

LOOK FOR:
1. Large white flamingo
2. Pale pink bill with black tip

NOTE: Young flamingoes of both
species have grey-brown plumage

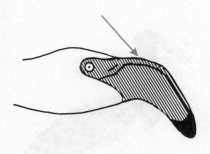

LESSER FLAMINGO

(*Newman's Birds* p. 82)

LOOK FOR:
1. Very pink flamingo
2. Dark red bill that looks
   black from a distance

WHITEFACED DUCK
(Newman's Birds p. 86)

LOOK FOR:
1. Black back of head, nape and upper neck
2. Chestnut-brown neck (not body)
3. Erect stance
4. All-dark wings in flight

SOUTH AFRICAN SHELDUCK (female)
(Newman's Birds p. 88)

LOOK FOR:
1. Grey back of head, crown and nape
2. Rest of bird chestnut-brown
3. Horizontal stance
4. White forewing and green secondary feathers in flight

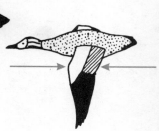

SOUTHERN POCHARD (female)

(Newman's Birds p. 90)

LOOK FOR:

1. Brown duck with white patch at bill base and white crescent shape from eye to throat
2. Blue-grey bill
3. High swimming posture
4. Tail held clear of water or trails

MACCOA DUCK (female)

(Newman's Birds p. 90)

LOOK FOR:

1. Small brown duck with horizontal pale and dark streaks on face
2. Dark grey bill
3. Low, squat posture on water
4. Tail trails in water or is held stiffly upwards

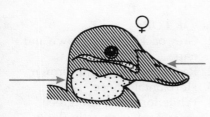

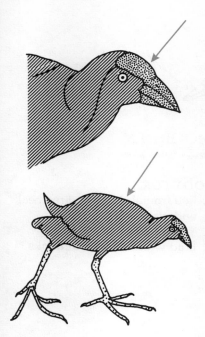

PURPLE GALLINULE

(Newman's Birds p. 98)

LOOK FOR:

1. Guineafowl-sized bird
2. Bright red frontal shield and beak
3. Pink legs
4. Bright blue, purple and green plumage

LESSER GALLINULE

(Newman's Birds p. 98)

LOOK FOR:

1. Dabchick-sized bird
2. Green, blue or grey frontal shield; red beak
3. Dull blue and green plumage

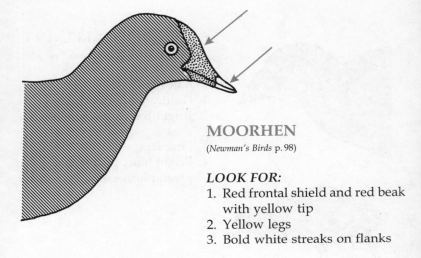

MOORHEN
(Newman's Birds p. 98)

LOOK FOR:
1. Red frontal shield and red beak with yellow tip
2. Yellow legs
3. Bold white streaks on flanks

NOTE: The Moorhen is a very common freshwater bird

LESSER MOORHEN
(Newman's Birds p. 98)

LOOK FOR:
1. Red frontal shield and red culmen on yellow beak
2. Dull pink or greenish legs
3. Lack of white flank streaks

NOTE: The Lesser Moorhen is uncommon and shy; skulks in waterside vegetation

WATTLED PLOVER

(Newman's Birds p. 122)

LOOK FOR:
1. White forehead and red frontal patch
2. Streaky neck
3. Grey underparts; breast to legs
4. Grey-brown wings

WHITECROWNED PLOVER

(Newman's Birds p. 122)

LOOK FOR:
1. White crown; beak to nape
2. Very long wattles
3. Entirely white underparts
4. Black and white wings

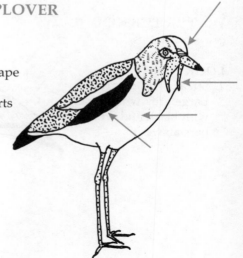

SPOTTED DIKKOP
(*Newman's Birds* p. 128)

LOOK FOR:
1. Very spotted upperparts
2. No wing-bar

NOTE: Both dikkops are nocturnal feeders. Spotted Dikkop occurs in dry, stony grassveld; Water Dikkop on banks of inland waters

WATER DIKKOP
(*Newman's Birds* p. 128)

LOOK FOR:
1. Streaky upperparts
2. Large grey wing panel with black and white bars above it

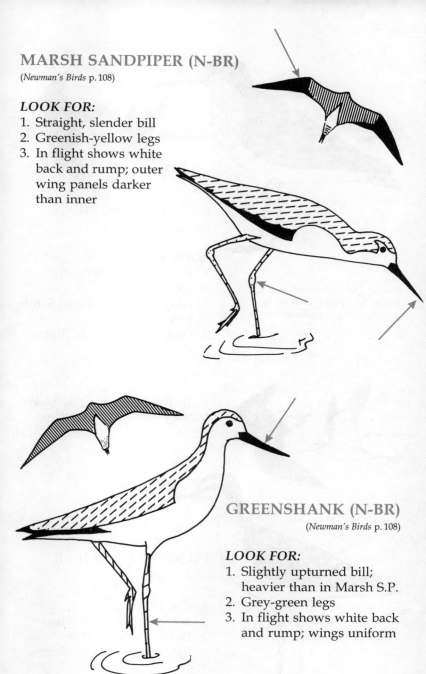

MARSH SANDPIPER (N-BR)
(*Newman's Birds* p. 108)

LOOK FOR:
1. Straight, slender bill
2. Greenish-yellow legs
3. In flight shows white back and rump; outer wing panels darker than inner

GREENSHANK (N-BR)
(*Newman's Birds* p. 108)

LOOK FOR:
1. Slightly upturned bill; heavier than in Marsh S.P.
2. Grey-green legs
3. In flight shows white back and rump; wings uniform

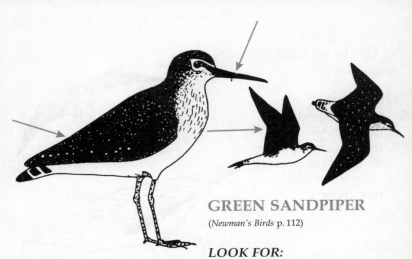

GREEN SANDPIPER
(*Newman's Birds* p. 112)

NOTE: The uncommon Green Sandpiper feeds in swiftly running streams

LOOK FOR:
1. Dark upperparts lightly spotted
2. Longer bill than Wood Sandpiper
3. Dark underwings in flight

NOTE: The common Wood Sandpiper feeds in the shallows of most inland waters

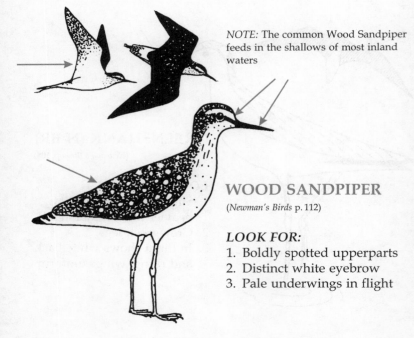

WOOD SANDPIPER
(*Newman's Birds* p. 112)

LOOK FOR:
1. Boldly spotted upperparts
2. Distinct white eyebrow
3. Pale underwings in flight

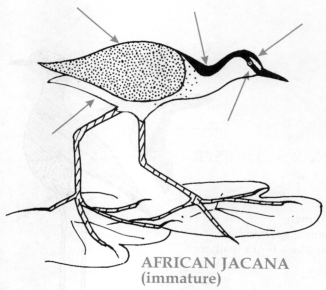

AFRICAN JACANA
(immature)
(Newman's Birds p. 118)

LOOK FOR:
1. Blackish eye-stripe, crown and hind neck
2. White eyebrow
3. Dull brown wings and back
4. White underparts (chestnut in adult) with yellow wash across breast

LESSER JACANA (adult)
(Newman's Birds p. 118)

LOOK FOR:
1. Diminutive size
2. Chestnut crown and eye-stripe with white eyebrow
3. Dark brown wings and back
4. White underparts; yellow wash from hind neck to wing fold

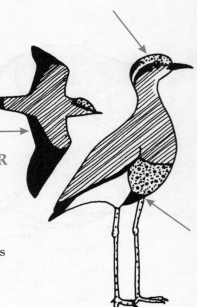

TEMMINCK'S COURSER
(*Newman's Birds* p. 130)

LOOK FOR:
1. Rufous crown
2. Black central spot on belly
3. In the air black flight feathers

BURCHELL'S COURSER
(*Newman's Birds* p. 130)

LOOK FOR:
1. Grey hind crown
2. Black bar on belly
3. In the air white bar on
   secondary wing feathers

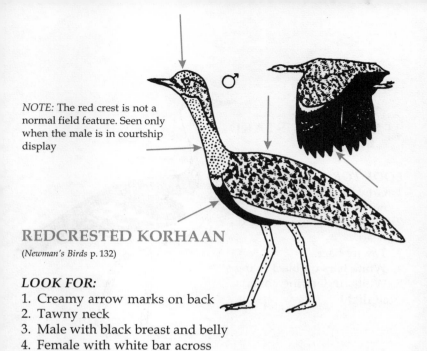

NOTE: The red crest is not a normal field feature. Seen only when the male is in courtship display

REDCRESTED KORHAAN

(*Newman's Birds* p. 132)

LOOK FOR:

1. Creamy arrow marks on back
2. Tawny neck
3. Male with black breast and belly
4. Female with white bar across breast plus black belly
5. Black wings in flight

NOTE: In comparison to the Redcrested Korhaan the Blackbellied appears longer in legs and neck

BLACKBELLIED KORHAAN

(*Newman's Birds* p. 136)

LOOK FOR:

1. Back spotted and barred
2. Male with black foreneck and belly
3. Female with fawn neck, white belly
4. White wings in flight

STANLEY'S BUSTARD

(Newman's Birds p. 134)

LOOK FOR:

1. Grey foreneck, rusty hind neck
2. Black and white streaked head
3. Tawny back
4. White bars on black wing
5. White underwing coverts in flight

KORI BUSTARD

(Newman's Birds p. 136)

LOOK FOR:

1. Greyish neck
2. Crest at back of head
3. Dark speckled back
4. Black breast band
5. Black spots on white wing
6. In flight underwing dark

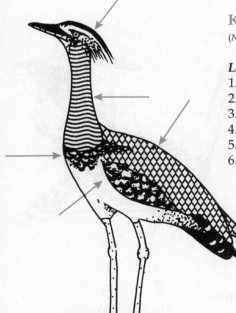

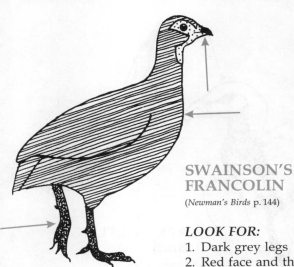

SWAINSON'S FRANCOLIN

(*Newman's Birds* p. 144)

LOOK FOR:

1. Dark grey legs
2. Red face and throat, black tip to bill
3. Plain, dark brown plumage

REDNECKED FRANCOLIN

(*Newman's Birds* p. 144)

LOOK FOR:

1. Red legs
2. Red face, bill and throat
3. Streaky underparts

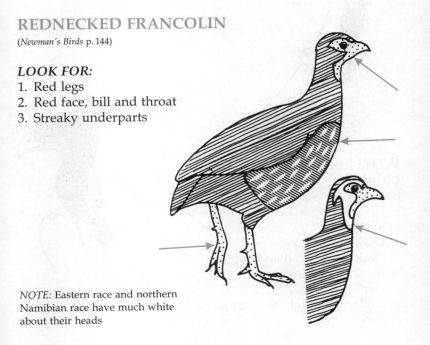

NOTE: Eastern race and northern Namibian race have much white about their heads

CAPE VULTURE
(adult)

(*Newman's Birds* p. 152)

LOOK FOR:
1. Pale appearance
2. White top to head and nape
3. Purple/red neck skin
4. Straw-coloured eye
5. In low flight pale secondaries are visible

WHITEBACKED VULTURE
(adult)

(*Newman's Birds* p. 152)

LOOK FOR:
1. Dark appearance
2. Dark top to head and nape
3. Blackish neck skin
4. Dark eye
5. Underwing flight feathers all dark

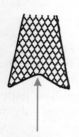

NOTE: Yellowbilled Kites occur in flocks at a food source, but otherwise occur singly. They breed in southern Africa.

YELLOWBILLED KITE
(*Newman's Birds* p. 158)

LOOK FOR:
1. Prominent yellow bill and cere (black bill in immatures)
2. Dark brown head and neck
3. Forked tail (less so when spread)

BLACK KITE
(*Newman's Birds* p. 158)

LOOK FOR:
1. Black bill; yellow cere
2. Grey head and neck
3. Tail less forked (square when spread)

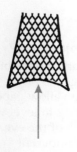

NOTE: Black Kites often move in flocks feeding on crop pests. They do not breed in southern Africa.

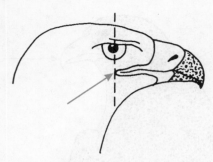

TAWNY EAGLE
(*Newman's Birds* p. 164)

LOOK FOR:
1. Pale buff or brown plumage
2. Pale yellow gape extending only to centre of eye
3. Undertail not barred

NOTE: The Tawny Eagle is a resident, breeding species

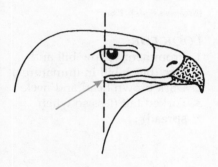

STEPPE EAGLE
(race A)
(*Newman's Birds* p. 164)

LOOK FOR:
1. Pale buff or dark brown plumage
2. Orange-yellow gape extends behind centre of eye but not to back of eye
3. Barred undertail

NOTE: Steppe Eagles are non-breeding summer visitors

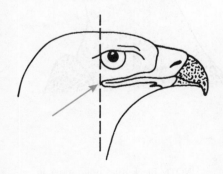

STEPPE EAGLE
(race B)
(*Newman's Birds* p. 164)

LOOK FOR:
1. Pale buff or dark brown plumage
2. Orange-yellow gape extending to level with the back of the eye
3. Barred undertail

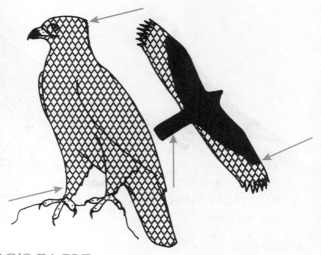

WAHLBERG'S EAGLE

(Newman's Birds p. 162)

LOOK FOR:
1. Small crest on head
2. Baggy leg feathers
3. In flight straight-edged wings and narrow, square tail

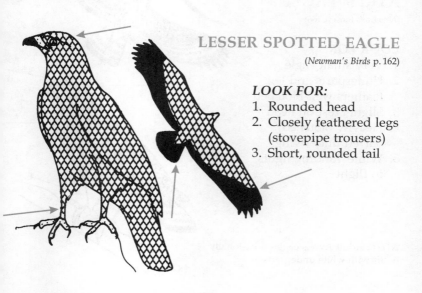

LESSER SPOTTED EAGLE

(Newman's Birds p. 162)

LOOK FOR:
1. Rounded head
2. Closely feathered legs (stovepipe trousers)
3. Short, rounded tail

AFRICAN HAWK EAGLE

(Newman's Birds p. 166)

LOOK FOR:

1. Medium-large eagle
2. White underparts moderately streaked
3. Leg feathers unstreaked
4. Pale windows in underwings
5. Dark trailing edge to white underwings and tail

AYRES' EAGLE

(Newman's Birds p. 166)

LOOK FOR:

1. Very small eagle
2. Underparts and leg feathers well blotched
3. Slight crest on head
4. Heavily blotched/ barred underwings
5. White 'landing lights' in flight

NOTE: Adult Ayre's eagles occasionally occur with white underparts

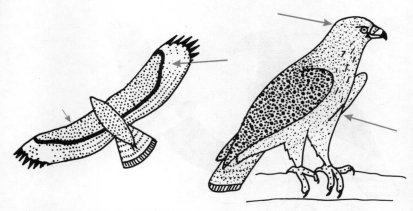

AFRICAN HAWK EAGLE (imm.)
(*Newman's Birds* p. 166)

LOOK FOR:
1. Medium sized eagle with rufous head and body
2. No crest on head
3. Rufous underwing coverts
4. Pale windows on underwing primaries

AYRES' EAGLE (imm.)
(*Newman's Birds* p. 166)

LOOK FOR:
1. Small eagle with pale rufous or nearly white underparts
2. Small crest on head
3. Rufous underwing coverts
4. Heavily blotched and barred primaries and secondaries

MARTIAL EAGLE
(*Newman's Birds* p. 168)

LOOK FOR:
1. Slightly crested head
2. Dark spots on white under-parts
3. Fully feathered legs
4. Dark underwings

BLACKBREASTED SNAKE EAGLE
(*Newman's Birds* p. 160)

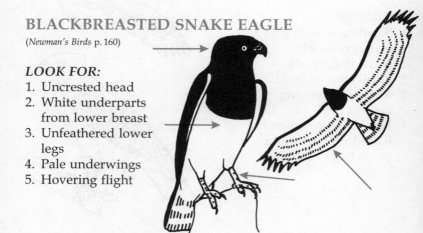

LOOK FOR:
1. Uncrested head
2. White underparts from lower breast
3. Unfeathered lower legs
4. Pale underwings
5. Hovering flight

PALE CHANTING GOSHAWK

(*Newman's Birds* p. 178)

LOOK FOR:

1. White on folded wing
2. In flight white on wing
3. White rump

NOTE: Pale Chanting has a westerly range

DARK CHANTING GOSHAWK

(*Newman's Birds* p. 178)

LOOK FOR:

1. Plain grey folded wing
2. In flight grey wing
3. Barred rump

NOTE: Dark Chanting has an easterly range

NOTE: European Marsh Harrier is a rare summer visitor

EUROPEAN MARSH HARRIER
(*Newman's Birds* p. 180)

IN MALE LOOK FOR:
1. Brown body
2. Grey on upper wings
3. Grey, unbarred tail
4. White on underwings

IN FEMALE LOOK FOR:
1. Brown body, wings and tail
2. Creamy crown, throat and pale-edged forewings

AFRICAN MARSH HARRIER
(*Newman's Birds* p. 182)

IN ADULT LOOK FOR:
1. Brown body
2. Brown upper wings
3. Brown, barred tail
4. Brown, barred underwing

IN IMMATURE LOOK FOR:
1. Whitish on edge of forewings
2. Dark body with pale chest-band
3. Pale underwing with dark barring and dark secondaries

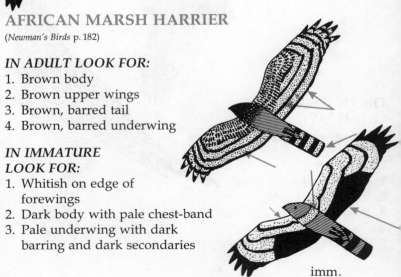

imm.

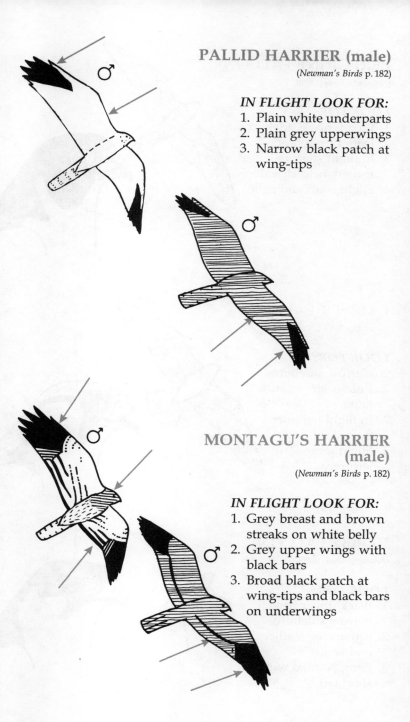

PALLID HARRIER (male)
(*Newman's Birds* p. 182)

IN FLIGHT LOOK FOR:
1. Plain white underparts
2. Plain grey upperwings
3. Narrow black patch at wing-tips

MONTAGU'S HARRIER (male)
(*Newman's Birds* p. 182)

IN FLIGHT LOOK FOR:
1. Grey breast and brown streaks on white belly
2. Grey upper wings with black bars
3. Broad black patch at wing-tips and black bars on underwings

PEREGRINE FALCON

(Newman's Birds p. 188)

LOOK FOR:

1. Broad, black sideburns
2. Dark upper head
3. In flight short tail usually held closed
4. Flight swift and agile

LANNER FALCON

(Newman's Birds p. 188)

LOOK FOR:

1. Narrow sideburns
2. Rufous crown and nape
3. In flight tail often fanned
4. Flight more leisurely

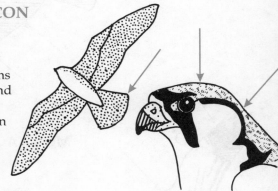

HOBBY FALCON

(Newman's Birds p. 188)

LOOK FOR:

1. Black upper head, narrow sideburns
2. Rufous leg feathers and vent
3. Long pointed wings, short tail

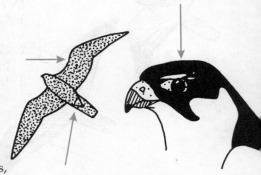

ROCK KESTREL
(Newman's Birds p. 192)

IN MALE LOOK FOR:
1. Grey head
2. Chestnut back with bold spots
3. Chestnut underparts with spots
4. Grey tail with black band
5. Pale underwing lightly barred

IN FEMALE LOOK FOR:
1. Grey head
2. Well barred grey tail

LESSER KESTREL
(Newman's Birds p. 192)

IN MALE LOOK FOR:
1. Grey head
2. Chestnut back, no spots
3. Pale underparts with small spots
4. Grey secondaries
5. Grey tail, black band
6. White underwings

IN FEMALE LOOK FOR:
1. Streaked head
2. White, streaked breast
3. Dull upperwings
4. Well barred brown tail

WESTERN REDFOOTED KESTREL

(Newman's Birds p. 192)

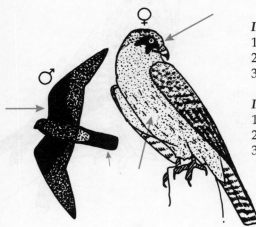

IN MALE LOOK FOR:
1. All dark grey plumage
2. Dark underwings
3. Dark grey undertail

IN FEMALE LOOK FOR:
1. Rufous head and body
2. Dark facial patch
3. Rufous underwing coverts

EASTERN REDFOOTED KESTREL

(Newman's Birds p. 192)

IN MALE LOOK FOR:
1. Pale grey body
2. White underwing coverts
3. Pale grey undertail

IN FEMALE LOOK FOR:
1. Dark crown plus white forehead
2. White throat and sides of head
3. Black blotches on white underparts
4. Underwings speckled black and white

BLUESPOTTED DOVE

(*Newman's Birds* p. 200)

LOOK FOR:
1. Red bill with yellow tip
2. Blue wing spots

EMERALDSPOTTED DOVE

(*Newman's Birds* p. 200)

LOOK FOR:
1. Black bill
2. Green wing spots

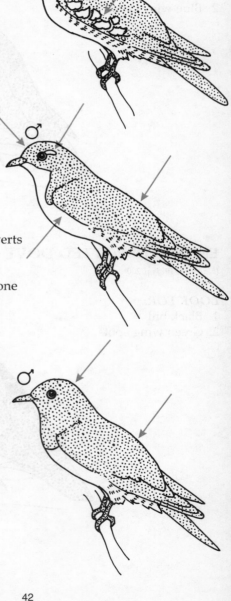

DIEDERIK CUCKOO
(male)

(Newman's Birds p. 208)

LOOK FOR:
1. Red eyes
2. White eyebrow from lores to ear coverts
3. White spots on wing
4. Broad bars on flanks

KLAAS'S CUCKOO
(male)

(Newman's Birds p. 208)

LOOK FOR:
1. Dark eyes
2. White mark over ear coverts only
3. Plain green wing
4. Thin bars on flanks or none at all

EMERALD CUCKOO
(male)

(Newman's Birds p. 208)

LOOK FOR:
1. Entirely green head, breast and upperparts
2. Yellow belly

DIEDERIK CUCKOO
(female)
(Newman's Birds p. 208)

LOOK FOR:
1. Red eye
2. Full white eyebrow
3. White spots on wing
4. Bronze sheen on mantle

KLAAS'S CUCKOO
(female)
(Newman's Birds p. 208)

LOOK FOR:
1. Dark eye
2. White spot over ear coverts
3. No white on wing
4. Well barred head, breast and flanks

EMERALD CUCKOO
(female)
(Newman's Birds p. 208)

LOOK FOR:
1. Bronze crown, wings and back
2. Close green barring over head, breast and upperparts
3. No white on wings
4. White on belly only

STRIPED CUCKOO

(*Newman's Birds* p. 208)

LOOK FOR:
Streaked breast

JACOBIN CUCKOO

(*Newman's Birds* p. 208)

LOOK FOR:
Plain white breast

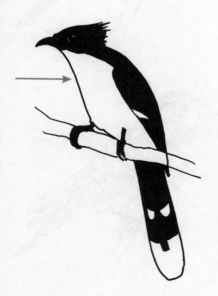

NOTE: Also occurs as
an all black form

BURCHELL'S COUCAL

(Newman's Birds p. 214)

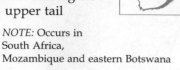

LOOK FOR:
Fine barring on
upper tail

NOTE: Occurs in
South Africa,
Mozambique and eastern Botswana

SENEGAL COUCAL

(Newman's Birds p. 214)

LOOK FOR:
Plain black tail

NOTE: Occurs in
Zimbabwe, northern
Botswana and northern Namibia

WHITEBROWED
COUCAL

(Newman's Birds p. 214)

LOOK FOR:
1. White eyebrow
   and white
   streaks on crown and mantle
2. Fine barring on upper tail

NOTE: Occurs in Zimbabwe, northern
Botswana and northern Namibia

COPPERYTAILED
COUCAL

(Newman's Birds p. 214)

LOOK FOR:
1. Purple sheen
   on head
2. Long coppery tail

NOTE: Occurs in northern Botswana

BARN OWL
(Newman's Birds p. 216)

LOOK FOR:
Pearl-grey upperparts with
chestnut markings

NOTE: Occurs everywhere

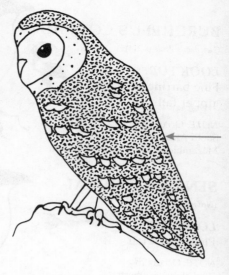

GRASS OWL
(Newman's Birds p. 216)

LOOK FOR:
Dark brown back

NOTE: Easterly range in moist
regions with long grass

PEARLSPOTTED OWL

(Newman's Birds p. 218)

LOOK FOR:
1. Small white spots on brown head and back
2. Brown-streaked underparts with white pearl-like spots
3. False eyes on back of head
4. Spotted tail

BARRED OWL

(Newman's Birds p. 218)

LOOK FOR:
1. Fine bars on brown head and back
2. Brown spots on white underparts
3. Barred tail

SPOTTED EAGLE OWL

(*Newman's Birds* p. 220)

LOOK FOR:

1. Pale yellow eyes
2. Lightly speckled breast
3. Fine bars on belly
4. Small feet and claws

CAPE EAGLE OWL

(*Newman's Birds* p. 220)

LOOK FOR:

1. Orange eyes
2. Dark blotched breast
3. Bold bars on belly
4. Large feet and claws

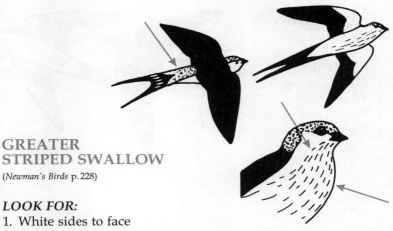

GREATER
STRIPED SWALLOW

(Newman's Birds p. 228)

LOOK FOR:
1. White sides to face
2. Light streaking below
3. Pale rump

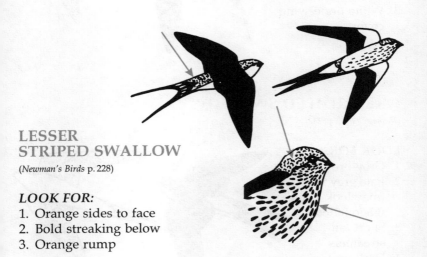

LESSER
STRIPED SWALLOW

(Newman's Birds p. 228)

LOOK FOR:
1. Orange sides to face
2. Bold streaking below
3. Orange rump

HOUSE MARTIN

(*Newman's Birds* p. 236)

LOOK FOR:
1. Dark blue cap
2. White rump
3. Forked tail, no streamers
4. Dark underwings

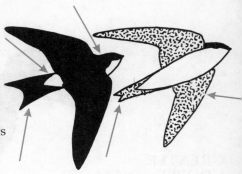

PEARLBREASTED SWALLOW

(*Newman's Birds* p. 232)

LOOK FOR:
1. Entirely dark blue upperparts
2. Forked tail, no streamers
3. White underwing coverts

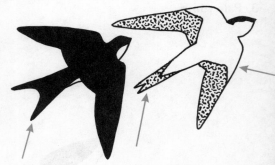

GREYRUMPED SWALLOW

(*Newman's Birds* p. 232)

LOOK FOR:
1. Grey-brown cap
2. Pale grey rump (may look white when faded)
3. Short tail streamers
4. Dark under-wings

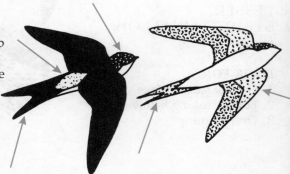

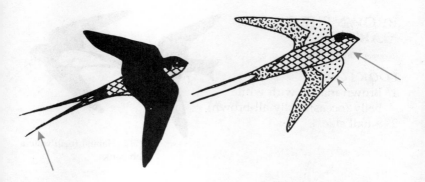

REDBREASTED SWALLOW

(*Newman's Birds* p. 228)

LOOK FOR:
1. Entirely orange below
2. Pale orange underwing coverts
3. Long tail streamers

MOSQUE SWALLOW

(*Newman's Birds* p. 228)

LOOK FOR:
1. White throat and upper breast
2. White underwing coverts
3. Short tail streamers

BROWNTHROATED MARTIN

(*Newman's Birds* p. 236)

LOOK FOR:
1. Brown martin with white belly (occasionally all-brown)
2. Small size

NOTE: Habitat fresh waters with banks

BANDED MARTIN

(*Newman's Birds* p. 236)

LOOK FOR:
1. Large size
2. Square tail
3. Broad breast-band on white body
4. White underwing coverts

ROCK MARTIN

(*Newman's Birds* p. 236)

LOOK FOR:
1. Dark brown upperparts
2. Paler brown body
3. Broad wings in flight

NOTE: Habitat rocky hills

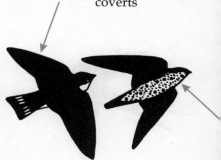

SAND MARTIN

(*Newman's Birds* p. 234)

LOOK FOR:
1. Small size
2. Forked tail
3. Narrow breast-band on white body
4. Dark underwings

NOTE: A summer visitor

BLACK SWIFT
(Newman's Birds p. 240)

LOOK FOR:
1. Well-forked tail
2. From above paler inner secondaries

NOTE: These two swifts can only be safely told apart under conditions of good light

EURASIAN SWIFT
(Newman's Birds p. 242)

LOOK FOR:
1. Shallow forked tail
2. Uniform black swift

WHITERUMPED SWIFT
(*Newman's Birds* p. 240)

LOOK FOR:
1. Well-forked tail
2. Small, crescent-shaped white rump
3. Slender body and wings

LITTLE SWIFT
(*Newman's Birds* p. 240)

LOOK FOR:
1. Square tail
2. Square white rump-patch that wraps over flanks
3. Dumpy appearance

HORUS SWIFT
(*Newman's Birds* p. 240)

LOOK FOR:
1. A Little Swift with a forked tail
2. Square white rump-patch
3. Robust build

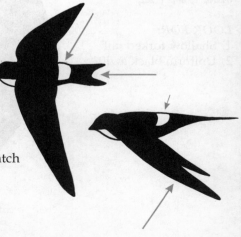

OLIVE BEE-EATER

(Newman's Birds p. 246)

LOOK FOR:
1. Brown crown
2. Rufous throat
3. Pale green underparts

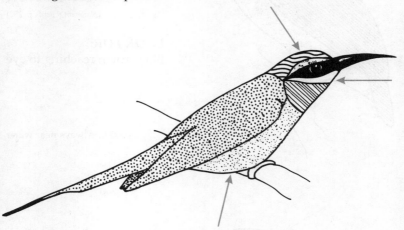

BLUECHEEKED BEE-EATER

(Newman's Birds p. 246)

LOOK FOR:
1. Green crown
2. Yellow chin
3. Brown chest and blue belly

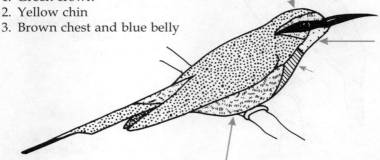

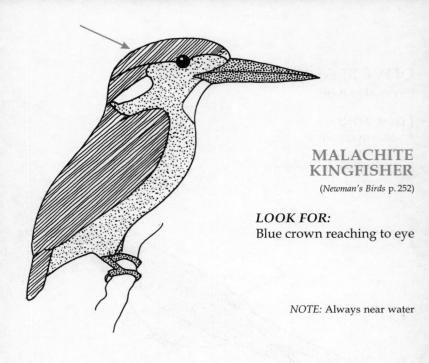

MALACHITE KINGFISHER

(Newman's Birds p. 252)

LOOK FOR:
Blue crown reaching to eye

NOTE: Always near water

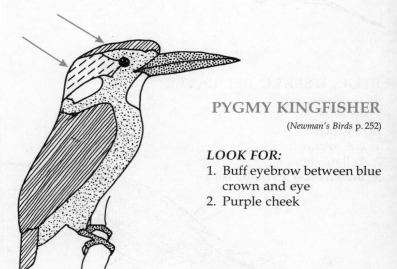

PYGMY KINGFISHER

(Newman's Birds p. 252)

LOOK FOR:
1. Buff eyebrow between blue crown and eye
2. Purple cheek

NOTE: Usually away from water

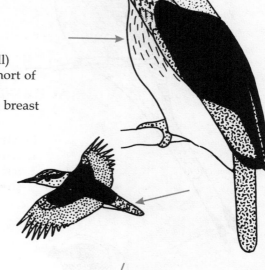

BROWNHOODED KINGFISHER
(Newman's Birds p. 252)

LOOK FOR:
1. Red bill (often dull)
2. Black eye-stripe short of nape
3. Chestnut wash on breast
4. Black rump

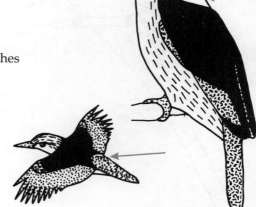

STRIPED KINGFISHER
(Newman's Birds p. 252)

LOOK FOR:
1. Red and black bill
2. Black eye-stripe reaches nape
3. White breast
4. Blue rump

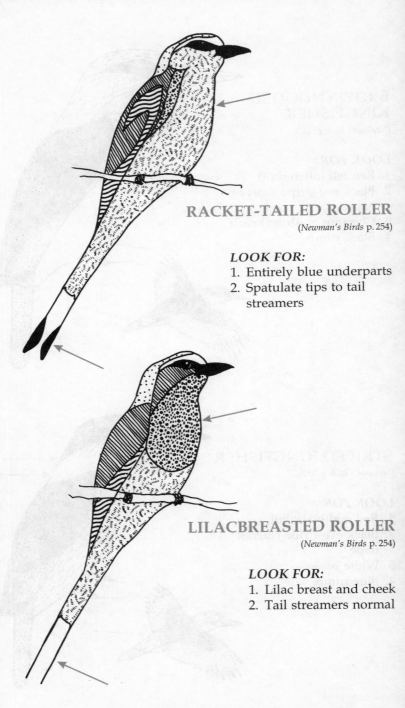

RACKET-TAILED ROLLER

(*Newman's Birds* p. 254)

LOOK FOR:
1. Entirely blue underparts
2. Spatulate tips to tail streamers

LILACBREASTED ROLLER

(*Newman's Birds* p. 254)

LOOK FOR:
1. Lilac breast and cheek
2. Tail streamers normal

SCIMITARBILLED WOODHOOPOE

(*Newman's Birds* p. 256)

LOOK FOR:

1. Well-decurved black bill
2. Black legs and feet
3. Small white bar on wing
4. Small white tail tips
5. Occurs singly or in pairs

imm.

REDBILLED WOODHOOPOE

(*Newman's Birds* p. 256)

LOOK FOR:

1. Red decurved bill, but black in immatures
2. Red legs and feet
3. Bold white wing-bars
4. Bold white tail tips
5. Occurs in noisy groups

CROWNED HORNBILL

(Newman's Birds p. 258)

LOOK FOR:
1. Red bill
2. Top of bill with casque
3. Dark brown head and back
4. Yellow line at base of bill

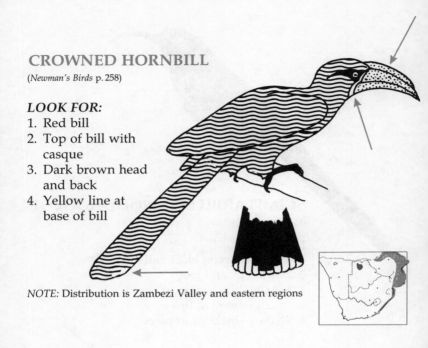

NOTE: Distribution is Zambezi Valley and eastern regions

BRADFIELD'S HORNBILL

(Newman's Birds p. 260)

LOOK FOR:
1. Orange-red bill
2. No casque on bill
3. Pale brown head and back
4. Lower breast and belly white

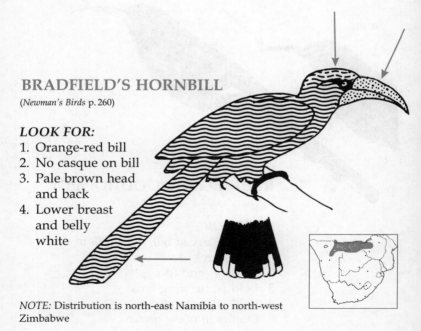

NOTE: Distribution is north-east Namibia to north-west Zimbabwe

SILVERYCHEEKED HORNBILL
(*Newman's Birds* p. 260)

LOOK FOR:
1. Huge size
2. Deep casque shorter than bill
3. Blue flesh around eye
4. Dark underparts to lower breast; white underbelly

NOTE: Distribution is eastern Zimbabwe and central Mozambique

TRUMPETER HORNBILL
(*Newman's Birds* p. 260)

LOOK FOR:
1. Large size
2. Casque length of bill in male; less in female
3. Pink flesh around eye
4. Upper breast dark, rest of underparts white

NOTE: Distribution is Zambezi Valley and eastern regions

SHARPBILLED
HONEYGUIDE

(*Newman's Birds* p. 272)

LOOK FOR:
1. Dark brown head and back
2. White throat
3. Dull edges to wing feathers

SLENDERBILLED
HONEYGUIDE

(*Newman's birds* p. 274)

LOOK FOR:
1. Greenish-brown back
2. Dark throat
3. Yellow-edged wing feathers

DUSKY LARK

(Newman's Birds p. 280)

LOOK FOR:
1. Dark brown crown and upperparts
2. Spots on breast only
3. Whitish legs

NOTE: Usually in loose flocks

SPOTTED THRUSH

(Newman's Birds p. 312)

LOOK FOR:
1. Grey-brown crown and upperparts
2. White bars on folded wing

NOTE: Occurs in understorey of evergreen coastal forests

GROUNDSCRAPER THRUSH

(Newman's Birds p. 312)

LOOK FOR:
1. Pale crown and upperparts
2. No white on wing

NOTE: Occurs in woodland, bushveld and suburbia

FORKTAILED DRONGO

(*Newman's Birds* p. 296)

LOOK FOR:
1. Distinctly forked tail
2. Dark red-brown eye
3. A noisy bird

NOTE: Occurs in any non-forest habitat with trees

SQUARETAILED DRONGO

(*Newman's Birds* p. 296)

LOOK FOR:
1. Tail with shallow fork
2. Wine-red eye
3. A noisy bird

NOTE: Occurs at edges of evergreen forests

BLACK FLYCATCHER

(*Newman's Birds* p. 296)

LOOK FOR:

1. Slight indentation in tail
2. A quiet bird
3. Dark brown eye

BLACK CUCKOOSHRIKE

(*Newman's Birds* p. 296)

IN MALE LOOK FOR:

1. Rounded tail
2. Orange-yellow gape
3. Yellow shoulder in some
4. A quiet bird

EUROPEAN GOLDEN ORIOLE

(*Newman's Birds* p. 302)

LOOK FOR:
1. Black wings
2. Short black eye-stripe

AFRICAN GOLDEN ORIOLE

(*Newman's Birds* p. 302)

LOOK FOR:
1. Yellow wings
2. Long black eye-stripe

ASHY GREY TIT

(*Newman's Birds* p. 308)

LOOK FOR:
1. White facial patch restricted to head
2. Blue-grey flanks

NOTE: Restricted to *Acacia* woodlands but very widespread

NORTHERN GREY TIT

(*Newman's Birds* p. 308)

LOOK FOR:
1. White facial patch extends down body
2. White flanks

NOTE: Restricted to Miombo woodlands of Zimbabwe

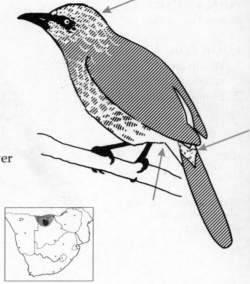

WHITERUMPED BABBLER

(*Newman's Birds* p. 310)

LOOK FOR:

1. Scaly appearance of white-edged head feathers
2. White rump and lower back
3. White belly blotched brown

NOTE: Restricted to Okavango Delta, Botswana and north western Zimbabawe

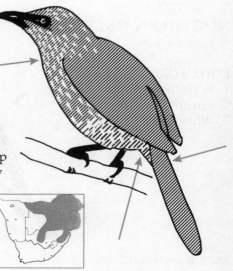

ARROWMARKED BABBLER

(*Newman's Birds* p. 310)

LOOK FOR:

1. White arrow marks on body, especially breast
2. Cinnamon-brown rump
3. Cinnamon-brown belly

KURRICHANE THRUSH

(*Newman's Birds* p. 312)

LOOK FOR:

1. Black moustacial stripe
2. White throat
3. Pale orange flanks and white belly

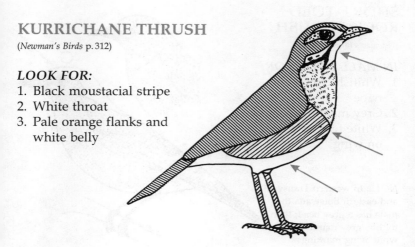

OLIVE THRUSH

(*Newman's Birds* p. 312)

LOOK FOR:

1. Speckled throat
2. Dull orange underparts and white vent

NOTE: Underparts are brighter orange in evergreen forests

SHORT-TOED ROCK THRUSH

(*Newman's Birds* p. 314)

IN MALE LOOK FOR:
1. Whitish crown and nape
2. Grey mantle
3. White feather edges on wing

NOTE: In western Transvaal and eastern Botswana the male has a grey head; then told by grey mantle and white wing markings

CAPE ROCK THRUSH

(*Newman's Birds* p. 314)

IN MALE LOOK FOR:
1. Grey head and neck
2. Orange-brown mantle
3. No white on wing

SENTINEL ROCK THRUSH

(*Newman's Birds* p. 314)

IN MALE LOOK FOR:
1. Grey head, mantle and upper breast
2. Underparts orange from lower breast only

NOTE: Range overlaps with Cape Rock Thrush only

SHORT-TOED ROCK THRUSH

(*Newman's Birds* p. 314)

IN FEMALE LOOK FOR:
1. White throat and white speckles on cheeks
2. Crown and mantle plain brown
3. Upper breast to belly orange (paler towards vent)

CAPE ROCK THRUSH

(*Newman's Birds* p. 314)

IN FEMALE LOOK FOR:
1. Brown speckled head
2. Rich orange breast
3. Pale-edged secondaries

SENTINEL ROCK THRUSH

(*Newman's Birds* p. 314)

IN FEMALE LOOK FOR:
1. Creamy throat and breast speckled brown
2. Lower breast only pale orange
3. Vent white

NOTE: Range overlaps with Cape Rock Thrush

WHITEBROWED ROBIN

(*Newman's Birds* p. 328)

LOOK FOR:
1. Streaked breast
2. Brown cap
3. Full white terminal
   band on tail

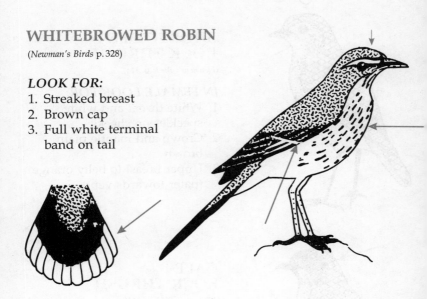

KALAHARI ROBIN

(*Newman's Birds* p. 330)

LOOK FOR:
1. Unstreaked breast
2. Grey cap
3. White tips to outer
   tail feathers only

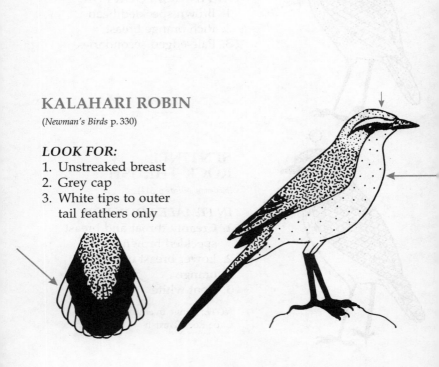

BARTHROATED APALIS

(Newman's Birds p. 340)

LOOK FOR:
1. No white eyebrow
2. Whitish eye
3. Grey to greenish upperparts
4. Belly yellow or white

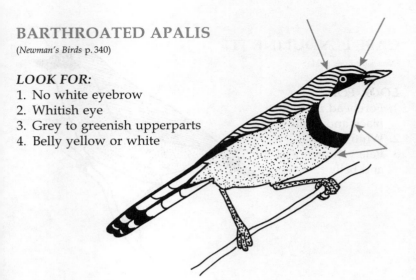

BLACKCHESTED PRINIA

(Newman's Birds p. 358)

LOOK FOR:
1. White eyebrow
2. Dark eye
3. Brown upperparts
4. Tail often raised
5. Throat and belly white

CAPE PENDULINE TIT

(Newman's Birds p. 344)

LOOK FOR:

1. Forehead mottled black and white
2. Whitish throat
3. Pale yellow breast and belly

GREY PENDULINE TIT

(Newman's Birds p. 344)

LOOK FOR:

1. Pale rufous forehead
2. White breast
3. Rufous belly and vent

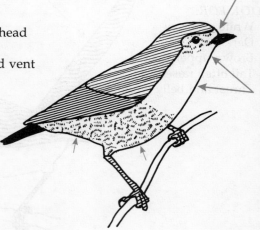

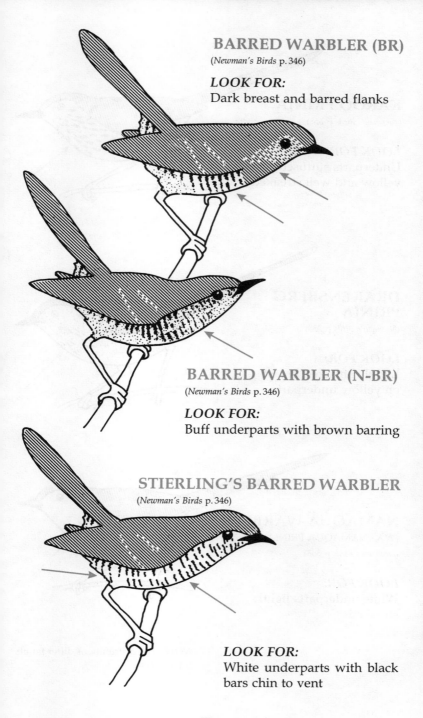

BARRED WARBLER (BR)
(*Newman's Birds* p. 346)

LOOK FOR:
Dark breast and barred flanks

BARRED WARBLER (N-BR)
(*Newman's Birds* p. 346)

LOOK FOR:
Buff underparts with brown barring

STIERLING'S BARRED WARBLER
(*Newman's Birds* p. 346)

LOOK FOR:
White underparts with black
bars chin to vent

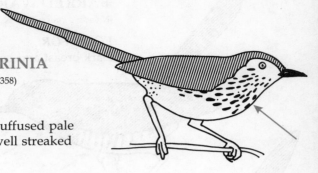

KAROO PRINIA

(*Newman's Birds* p. 358)

LOOK FOR:
Underparts suffused pale
yellow and well streaked

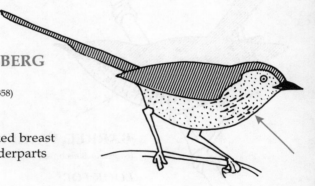

DRAKENSBERG PRINIA

(*Newman's Birds* p. 358)

LOOK FOR:
Lightly streaked breast
on yellow underparts

NAMAQUA WARBLER
(WAS NAMAQUA PRINIA)

(*Newman's Birds* p. 358)

LOOK FOR:
White underparts lightly
streaked

NOTE: The distributions differ for all
three species

DUSKY FLYCATCHER

(*Newman's Birds* p. 362)

LOOK FOR:
1. Dark, dumpy appearance
2. Dusky underparts with faint smudges on breast

NOTE: Edges of evergreen forests, riverine forests and kloofs

SPOTTED FLYCATCHER

(*Newman's Birds* p. 362)

LOOK FOR:
1. Whitish underparts
2. Streaked crown
3. Streaked breast and flanks

NOTE: Woodland, bushveld and wooded suburbia

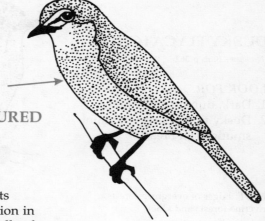

MOUSECOLOURED FLYCATCHER

(*Newman's Birds* p. 362)

LOOK FOR:
1. Dusky underparts
2. Eastern distribution in broadleafed woodland

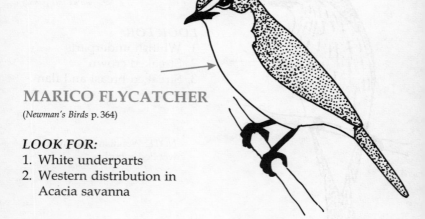

MARICO FLYCATCHER

(*Newman's Birds* p. 364)

LOOK FOR:
1. White underparts
2. Western distribution in Acacia savanna

FANTAILED FLYCATCHER

(Newman's Birds p. 362)

LOOK FOR:

1. White outer tail feathers
2. Active in trees, always fanning its tail

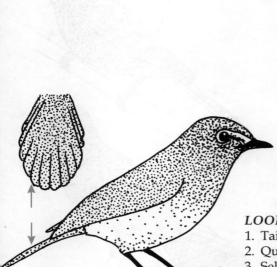

BLUEGREY FLYCATCHER

(Newman's Birds p. 362)

LOOK FOR:

1. Tail without any white
2. Quiet, still-hunter
3. Seldom fans tail

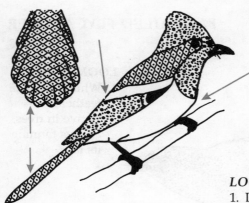

BLUEMANTLED FLYCATCHER

(*Newman's Birds* p. 368)

LOOK FOR:
1. Dark breast, white belly
2. White wing-bar
3. No white on tail

WHITETAILED FLYCATCHER

(*Newman's Birds* p. 368)

LOOK FOR:
1. All-dark underparts
2. No white on wing
3. White outer tail feathers

NOTE: Eastern
Zimbabwe/Mozambique
border only

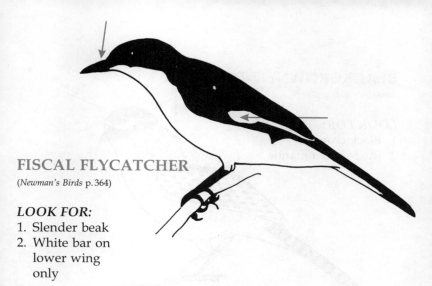

FISCAL FLYCATCHER

(*Newman's Birds* p. 364)

LOOK FOR:

1. Slender beak
2. White bar on lower wing only

FISCAL SHRIKE

(*Newman's Birds* p. 372)

LOOK FOR:

1. Heavy, hooked beak
2. White wing-bar extends to shoulder

81

BLACKCROWNED TCHAGRA

(*Newman's Birds* p. 376)

LOOK FOR:
1. Black crown
2. Rust-brown mantle

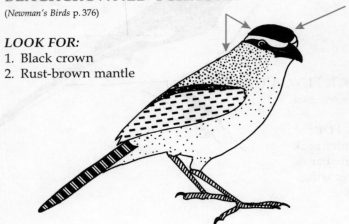

THREESTREAKED TCHAGRA

(*Newman's Birds* p. 376)

LOOK FOR:
1. Grey-brown crown
2. Grey-brown mantle

LONGTAILED GLOSSY STARLING

(Newman's Birds p. 384)

LOOK FOR:
1. Long, graduated tail
2. No black ear-patch
3. Wing-tips reach base of tail

BURCHELL'S GLOSSY STARLING

(Newman's Birds p. 384)

LOOK FOR:
1. 'Normal' straight tail
2. Black ear-patch present
3. Wing-tips reach halfway down tail

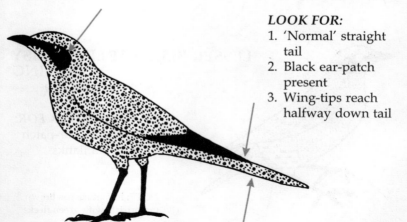

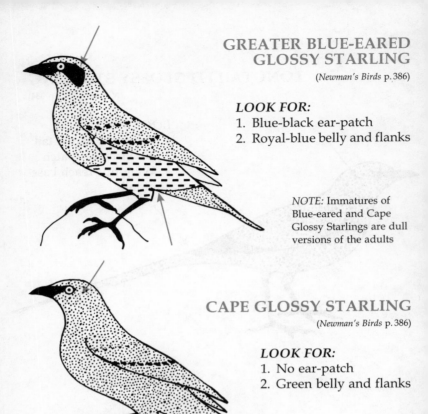

GREATER BLUE-EARED GLOSSY STARLING

(Newman's Birds p. 386)

LOOK FOR:
1. Blue-black ear-patch
2. Royal-blue belly and flanks

NOTE: Immatures of
Blue-eared and Cape
Glossy Starlings are dull
versions of the adults

CAPE GLOSSY STARLING

(Newman's Birds p. 386)

LOOK FOR:
1. No ear-patch
2. Green belly and flanks

LESSER BLUE-EARED GLOSSY STARLING

(Newman's Birds p. 386)

IN ADULT LOOK FOR:
1. Blue-black ear-patch
2. Magenta flanks

NOTE: Immature has brown
underparts with green flecks;
the eye dull

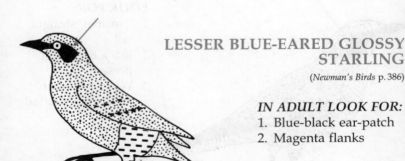

GREATER DOUBLECOLLARED SUNBIRD

(Newman's Birds p.392)

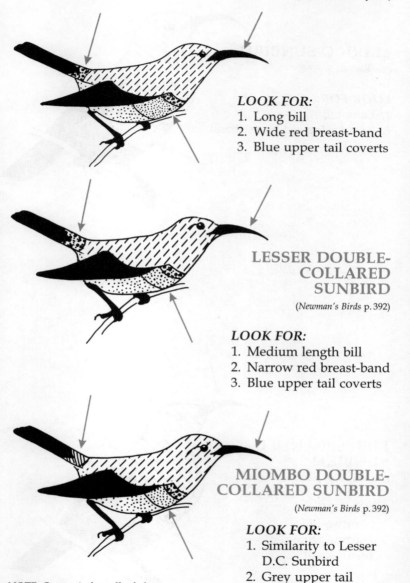

LOOK FOR:
1. Long bill
2. Wide red breast-band
3. Blue upper tail coverts

LESSER DOUBLE-COLLARED SUNBIRD

(Newman's Birds p.392)

LOOK FOR:
1. Medium length bill
2. Narrow red breast-band
3. Blue upper tail coverts

MIOMBO DOUBLE-COLLARED SUNBIRD

(Newman's Birds p.392)

LOOK FOR:
1. Similarity to Lesser D.C. Sunbird
2. Grey upper tail coverts

NOTE: Occurs in broadleafed woodland in Zimbabwe only

85

MARICO SUNBIRD

(*Newman's Birds* p. 398)

LOOK FOR:
1. Long bill
2. Broad wine-red breast-band

PURPLEBANDED SUNBIRD

(*Newman's Birds* p. 398)

LOOK FOR:
1. Shortish bill
2. Narrow wine-red breast-band

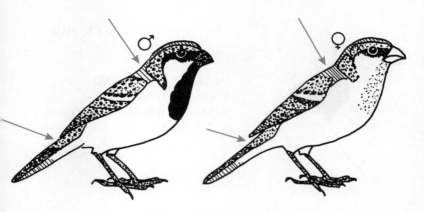

GREAT SPARROW
(Newman's Birds p. 406)

IN MALE LOOK FOR:
1. Large sparrow
2. Chestnut-brown on sides of head and mantle
3. Chestnut rump

IN FEMALE LOOK FOR:
1. Large sparrow
2. Bright chestnut on wings and rump

NOTE: The Great Sparrow is found away from human habitation in dry thornveld

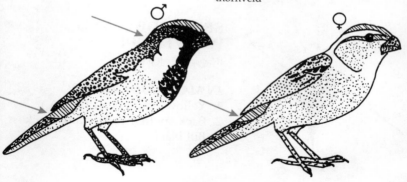

HOUSE SPARROW
(Newman's Birds p. 404)

IN MALE LOOK FOR:
1. Small sparrow
2. Red-brown on sides of head and mantle
3. Grey rump

IN FEMALE LOOK FOR:
1. Small sparrow
2. Drab grey and pale brown appearance

NOTE: The House Sparrow associates with human habitation

MASKED WEAVER (BR)

(Newman's Birds p. 412)

IN MALE LOOK FOR:
1. Orange-red eye
2. Mask extends over forehead
3. Bill black

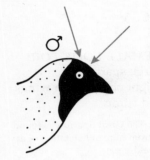

LESSER MASKED WEAVER (BR)

(Newman's Birds p. 412)

IN MALE LOOK FOR:
1. Pale yellow eye
2. Mask extends over top of head
3. Bill black

SPOTTEDBACKED WEAVER (BR)

(Newman's Birds p. 412)

IN MALE LOOK FOR:
1. Yellow top to head (in S.A.)
2. Back spotted yellow and black
3. Bill black

NOTE: Males have black heads in Zimbabwe and northern Botswana

MASKED WEAVER (BR)
(Newman's Birds p. 412)

IN FEMALE LOOK FOR:
1. Brown eye
2. Breast buff, belly white
3. Bill pinkish-horn

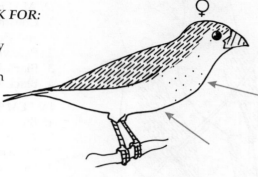

LESSER MASKED WEAVER (BR)
(Newman's Birds p. 412)

IN FEMALE LOOK FOR:
1. Pale yellow or brown eye
2. Yellow underparts
3. Bill pinkish-horn

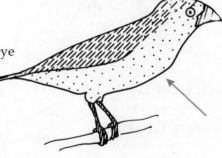

SPOTTEDBACKED WEAVER (BR)
(Newman's Birds p. 412)

IN FEMALE LOOK FOR:
1. Yellow breast
2. White belly
3. Bill pinkish-horn

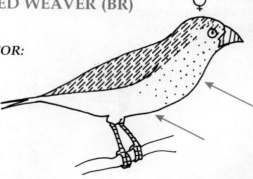

CAPE WEAVER (BR)

(*Newman's Birds* p. 408)

IN MALE LOOK FOR:
1. Chestnut wash over head and throat
2. Pale yellow or white eye
3. Black lores
4. Black bill

IN FEMALE LOOK FOR:
1. Buff throat and breast
2. White belly
3. Brown eye
4. Horn-coloured bill

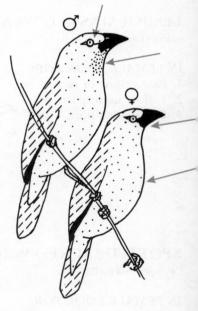

GOLDEN WEAVER (BR)

(*Newman's Birds* p. 410)

IN MALE LOOK FOR:
1. Chestnut wash on throat only
2. Pale yellow eye
3. Golden appearance
4. Black bill

IN FEMALE LOOK FOR:
1. Yellow underparts
2. Pale yellow eye
3. Black bill

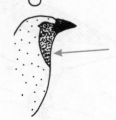

BROWNTHROATED WEAVER (BR)

(*Newman's Birds* p. 410)

IN MALE LOOK FOR:
1. Small size
2. Brown patch eye to throat
3. Black bill

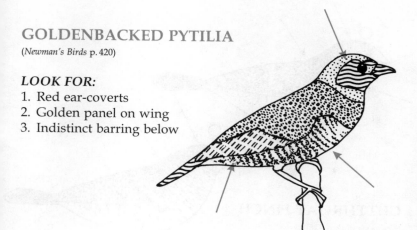

GOLDENBACKED PYTILIA
(*Newman's Birds* p. 420)

LOOK FOR:
1. Red ear-coverts
2. Golden panel on wing
3. Indistinct barring below

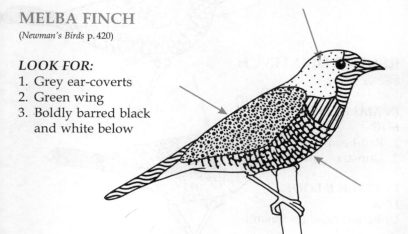

MELBA FINCH
(*Newman's Birds* p. 420)

LOOK FOR:
1. Grey ear-coverts
2. Green wing
3. Boldly barred black
   and white below

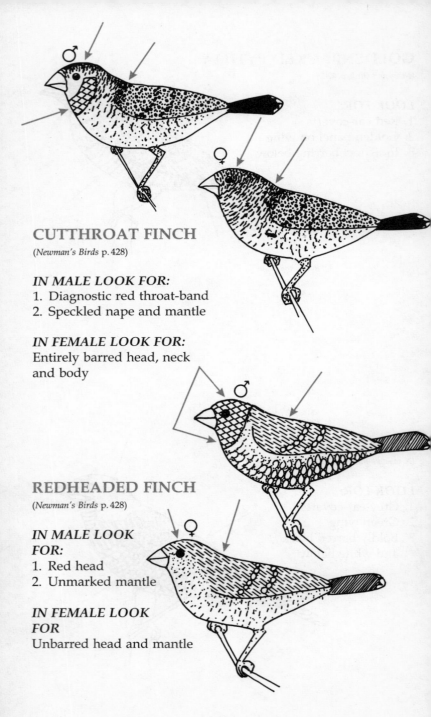

CUTTHROAT FINCH

(*Newman's Birds* p. 428)

IN MALE LOOK FOR:
1. Diagnostic red throat-band
2. Speckled nape and mantle

IN FEMALE LOOK FOR:
Entirely barred head, neck and body

REDHEADED FINCH

(*Newman's Birds* p. 428)

IN MALE LOOK FOR:
1. Red head
2. Unmarked mantle

IN FEMALE LOOK FOR
Unbarred head and mantle

BRONZE MANNIKIN
(*Newman's Birds* p. 430)

LOOK FOR:
1. Black and whitish bill
2. Dull brown nape
3. Dull brown back
4. Barred flanks

REDBACKED MANNIKIN
(*Newman's Birds* p. 430)

LOOK FOR:
1. Whitish bill
2. Black nape
3. Red-brown back
4. Mottled flanks

GOLDENBREASTED BUNTING

(*Newman's Birds* p. 442)

LOOK FOR:
1. White cheek-stripe
2. Red-brown back
3. Yellow underparts
   with orange breast

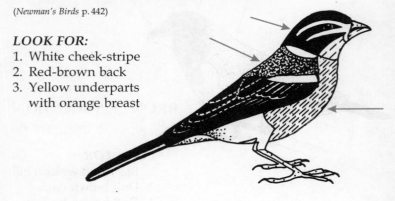

CABANIS'S BUNTING

(*Newman's Birds* p. 442)

LOOK FOR:
1. No cheek-stripe
2. Grey back
3. Yellow underparts

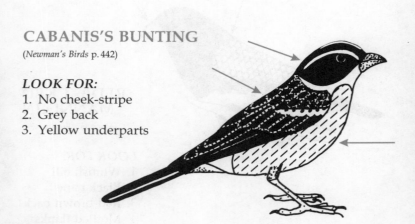

NOTE: Occurs in Miombo woodland

INDEX

Klaas's Cuckoo (female) 43
Klaas's Cuckoo (male) 42
Kori Bustard 26
Kurrichane Thrush 69

Lanner Falcon 38
Lesser Blue-eared Glossy Starling 84
Lesser Doublecollared Sunbird 85
Lesser Flamingo 14
Lesser Gallinule 17
Lesser Jacana (adult) 23
Lesser Kestrel 39
Lesser Masked Weaver (BR)
  (female) 89
Lesser Masked Weaver (BR) (male) 88
Lesser Moorhen 18
Lesser Spotted Eagle 31
Lesser Striped Swallow 49
Lilacbreasted Roller 58
Little Bittern (female) 9
Little Bittern (male) 9
Little Swift 54
Longtailed Glossy Starling 83

Maccoa Duck (female) 16
Malachite Kingfisher 56
Marico Flycatcher 78
Marico Sunbird 86
Marsh Sandpiper (N-BR) 21
Martial Eagle 34
Masked Weaver (BR) (female) 89
Masked Weaver (BR) (male) 88
Melba Finch 91
Miombo Doublecollared Sunbird 85
Montagu's Harrier (male) 37
Moorhen 18
Mosque Swallow 51
Mousecoloured Flycatcher 78

Namaqua Warbler 76
Northern Grey Tit 67

Olive Bee-eater 55
Olive Thrush 69

Pale Chanting Goshawk 35
Pallid Harrier (male) 37
Pearlbreasted Swallow 50
Pearlspotted Owl 47
Peregrine Falcon 38
Pinkbacked Pelican 5
Purple Gallinule 17
Purplebanded Sunbird 86
Pygmy Kingfisher 56

Racket-tailed Roller 58

Redbacked Mannikin 93
Redbilled Woodhoopoe 59
Redbreasted Swallow 51
Redcrested Korhaan 25
Redheaded Finch 92
Rednecked Francolin 27
Reed Cormorant 7
Rock Kestrel 39
Rock Martin 52
Rufousbellied Heron 10

Sand Martin 52
Scimitarbilled Woodhoopoe 59
Senegal Coucal 45
Sentinel Rock Thrush (female) 71
Sentinel Rock Thrush (male) 70
Sharpbilled Honeyguide 62
Short-toed Rock Thrush (female) 71
Short-toed Rock Thrush (male) 70
Silverycheeked Hornbill 61
Slaty Egret 10
Slenderbilled Honeyguide 62
South African Shelduck (female) 15
Southern Pochard (female) 16
Spotted Dikkop 20
Spotted Eagle Owl 48
Spotted Flycatcher 77
Spotted Thrush 63
Spottedbacked Weaver (BR)
  (female) 89
Spottedbacked Weaver (BR) (male) 88
Squaretailed Drongo 64
Stanley's Bustard 26
Steppe Eagle (race A) 30
Steppe Eagle (race B) 30
Stierling's Barred Warbler 75
Striped Cuckoo 44
Striped Kingfisher 57
Swainson's Francolin 27

Tawny Eagle 30
Temminck's Courser 24
Threestreaked Tchagra 82
Trumpeter Hornbill 61

Wahlberg's Eagle 31
Water Dikkop 20
Wattled Plover 19
Western Redfooted Kestrel 40
Whiskered Tern (N-BR) 4
White Pelican 5
Whitebacked Vulture (adult) 28
Whitebreasted Cormorant 7
Whitebrowed Coucal 45
Whitebrowed Robin 72
Whitecrowned Plover 19